Cindi Reeve

DIX TABLEAUX

A Play in Ten Scenes

by

Mark Dunn

SAMUEL FRENCH, INC.

45 West 25th Street
NEW YORK 10010
LONDON

7623 Sunset Boulevard
HOLLYWOOD 90046
TORONTO

ISBN 978 0 573 63397 3 Printed in U.S.A. #387

IMPORTANT BILLING AND CREDIT REQUIREMENTS

All producers of **DIX TABLEAUX** must give credit to the Author of the Play in all programs distributed in connection with performances of the Play, and in all instances in which the title of the Play appears for the purposes of advertising, publicizing or otherwise exploiting the Play and /or a production. The name of the Author must appear on a separate line on which no other name appears, immediately following the title and must appear in size of type not less than fifty percent of the size of the title type.

DIX TABLEAUX opened at the Community Theatre League in Williamsport, Pennsylvania on January 21, 2005. The director was Tom Ryersbach. The producer was Jeane Ryersbach. The set design was by Scott Palmer. The lighting designer and technical director was Perry Costello. The chief costumer was Gail Landers. The chief wardrobe mistress was Nancy Reiff. The props chief was Bonnie Brown. The hair stylist was Kelly A. Masteller. The stage manager was Jessica Orso. The assistant stage manager was Salem Bryant. The three principle actors, in order of appearance were:

BEVERLY	Andrée Phillips
ADDIE	Sandie Fairman
MAUREEN	Susan Guinter

The "promenaders" were, in alphabetical order:

CHERYL APPLETON, DANIELLE CLEARY, TAMARA CLEMENTS, JANICE COSTELLO, PERRY COSTELLO, SANDRA DOUGHERTY, JUSTYNE FREDERICK, STEVE HAMOD, JOSHUA LLOYD, JANET NASH, KASSANDRA NASH, VALERIE NEIDIG, CONDE PEOPLES, MACKENZIE RUBY, LAURA WALTZ, GERTRUDE WARD, and KEN WELSH

CHARACTER AND CASTING NOTES

DIX TABLEAUX was written to be performed by a variable number of actors. However, the three principal roles should not be multiply-cast. Both of the two main characters ADDIE SPOOL and BEVERLY DUGGINS will, in first scene, be sixty-one years of age and by the end of the play will have aged to seventy. The role of MAUREEN should be played by a woman in her middle years.

The remaining members of the cast will play the PROMENADERS, an eclectic bunch of men, women and children who stroll in and out of the play making commentary on the tableaux that have been assembled for their enjoyment. The author has written these roles to be played most economically by two women, one young and one middle aged; a middle-aged man; and a young girl of elementary school age. In productions in which economy of casting is not an issue, the author grants permission to cast these roles however best suits the production, even altering age and sex when necessary to spread the roles among a large ensemble. The additional role of NURSE may be cast separately or doubled by one of the actors playing promenaders.

The actors playing promenaders will also be enlisted to fill seats in the final funeral tableaux.

TIME AND PLACE

The play is divided into ten scenes, all but one taking place on a Saturday at roughly the same time in late spring in consecutive years. It begins in the recent past and proceeds into the present. The play takes place in the city of Dix, a medium-sized municipality found somewhere in the (not too deep) American South and in New York City.

STAGING NOTE

DIX TABLEAUX may be performed with or without an intermission. If an intermission is desired it would work best between the fifth and sixth tableaux (the school classroom and the shoe store).

for
Andrée Phillips

(LIGHTS come up in a museum gallery. Paintings have been removed from its walls; perhaps there are various-sized rectangular discolorations marking the wall space where they previously hung. Display cases have been removed or pushed back to allow room for the following: a platformed "tableau," or piece of living statuary — a moment of history captured and realized by the frozen poses of one ADDIE SPOOL and one BEVERLY DUGGINS, both women amply, even comically, dressed in 19th century frontier garb, including bonnets and aprons, flouncy blouses and long utilitarian skirts. ADDIE is stooped slightly over a butter churn. BEVERLY is frozen in her chore of beating a large rug with a broom. The two women remain stock-still. Not terribly convincing as statues, they do their best to effect the effect, despite a nose itch here, a muffled cough there. TWO FEMALE PROMENADERS ENTER. They stand before the tableau, smile and nod their approval, then move on. A moment or so passes. We hear the muffled RING of a cell phone. BEVERLY reacts to it, looks about to make sure the coast is clear, then pulls it from her apron pocket and places it to her ear. ADDIE doesn't break her pose, but her eyes cut over to BEVERLY. SHE regards her for the moment with obvious interest.)

BEVERLY. Hello? ... Yes, of course I'm here. Everything's fine. I told you: I don't mind. Really, dear, I do not mind. I'm having fun. It's fun, it really is. *(Beat; a decided change of tone.)* So when do I get to go home?... No, no, I'm just curious. There's no need to worry. Stop worrying about me. Bye, dear.

(SHE hangs up the phone and returns it in her pocket. SHE resumes her pose. Beat.)

ADDIE. You're not supposed to take phone calls.
BEVERLY. That was my son.
ADDIE. People didn't have cell phones in 1876.
BEVERLY. He was checking up on me.
ADDIE. They may have had cups with string.
BEVERLY. *(After a beat.)* Can we switch places?
ADDIE. You mean right now?
BEVERLY. Yes.
ADDIE. You're tired of beating the rug? You'd rather churn the butter?
BEVERLY. *(Nodding.)* My arm is starting to ache a little. It tends to do that when I hold it over my head for long periods of time.
ADDIE. We're allowed to rest between promenaders.
BEVERLY. We are?
ADDIE. Yes.
BEVERLY. Thank *God!*

(BEVERLY lowers the arm which had been holding the broom. SHE begins to massage it.)

ADDIE. But we have to be vigilant.

(ADDIE pulls herself up and stretches her back.)

BEVERLY. What do you mean?

ADDIE. In case anybody comes.

BEVERLY. So — should we take turns being on the look-out?

ADDIE. That sounds like a good plan. I'll go first.

(She keeps her eyes peeled for approaching promenaders.)

BEVERLY. Things were so rushed earlier. I've already forgotten your —

ADDIE. *(Offering her hand to shake.)* Addie. Addie Spool. Like a spool of thread.

BEVERLY. *(Shaking.)* We really didn't get a proper introduction, did we, Addie?

ADDIE. Well, you missed the orientation. *(Beat.)* There was coffee. *(Beat.)* And turnovers.

BEVERLY. I was a last minute replacement.

ADDIE. You're Beverly.

BEVERLY. Yes. Beverly.

ADDIE. Brian's mother.

BEVERLY. Yes. Brian's mother. *(Beat.)* That was Brian on the phone.

ADDIE. He's doing very well.

BEVERLY. *(With a mother's pride.)* You think so, really? This being his first year, he wants very badly for everything to go well. He says nobody does these tableaux anymore. It's not an easy sort of thing to pull off.

ADDIE. I guess you can say we're sort of locked into a tradition here. It's a part of the town heritage.

BEVERLY. Yes, that's what I understand.

ADDIE. They used to be very popular, you know.

BEVERLY *(Nodding.)* How long have *you* been —

ADDIE. *(Detecting someone, to BEVERLY.)* Pose! Pose!

(The TWO WOMEN suspend their conversation and resume their poses. A WOMAN, MAN and YOUNG GIRL enter and stop in front of the tableau. The GIRL touches the butter churn.)

WOMAN. Don't touch the tableau, dear. *(To ADDIE.)* Sorry about touching the churn, frontier lady.

GIRL. That isn't a frontier lady. It's Miss Spool from the drug store. Hello, Miss Spool.

(ADDIE doesn't respond. She stares ahead, as poker-faced as she is able.)

MAN. Don't pester the pharmacy lady, Tamara.

WOMAN. *(To BEVERLY.)* I don't know you. *(BEVERLY also looks impassively ahead.)* You're good though. You're very good. Look, Roger. Look how still she is. She looks almost lifelike.

(Something catches TAMARA's eye in the next room and she runs on ahead.)

WOMAN. *(Cont.)* Tamara, don't run. This is a museum. Slow down, young lady!

(They move on. After their EXIT, ADDIE and BEVERLY relax.)

ADDIE. So what was it you —

(Apparently seeing someone else coming, SHE straightens back up. A WOMAN enters alone. She stops in front of the tableau, looks down at the museum guide which she holds in her hand.)

WOMAN. *(Reading aloud.)* "The daily work of the women folk

was never done. In addition to hard field labor at the side of her husband, a frontier wife was expected to spend her remaining hours cooking and cleaning and tending the 'young-un's.' The drudgery was seldom relieved in this era of few household conveniences. Today these women would engage a babysitter and a housekeeper, then be off to a fitting or an afternoon with the 'girls.'" *(To herself.)* "Afternoon with the —" Who wrote this stuff? *(To ADDIE.)* Addie, I need a refill on my Fosamax. *(To BEVERLY.)* I don't know you.

(SHE goes. Again, ADDIE and BEVERLY relax. ADDIE pulls out a little note pad and writes something down.)

ADDIE. I wish people wouldn't give me their pharmacy orders. That's five already. I'm supposed to be a frontier wife. I'm supposed to be making butter.

BEVERLY. May I say something honestly?

ADDIE. Of course you can, honey.

BEVERLY. This is the stupidest way to raise money for a museum I can imagine.

ADDIE. They've been doing it for ninety-seven years. Every year, except 1918.

BEVERLY. What happened in 1918?

ADDIE. There was a controversy. They had to cancel it.

BEVERLY. A controversy? What kind of a controversy?

ADDIE. The museum director wanted a tableau of a German Hun chasing a Belgian child with a bayonet. A lot of people thought that was going a little too far.

BEVERLY. Yes. I can see that. You were going to tell me —

ADDIE. Oh yes. Thirty-three years. 'Haven't missed a single one. I've played school teachers and farmers' wives and a mother of the bride and a librarian and a nurse and a tornado victim and two years ago I played a dance hall floozie. People got upset because they thought I was a prostitute. Well, as you can imagine, I was very offended by such talk. I said — and this is the only time I've had a word with any of the promenaders — I said if you think *I'm* a hooker, then I guess Miss Kitty's a hooker too. Do you think Miss Kitty's a hooker? Do *you* think Marshal Dillon shares Miss Kitty's womb with every Tom, Dick and Harry who comes riding into Dodge City?

BEVERLY. *(After a beat.)* What on earth are you talking about?

ADDIE. Gunsmoke. *(Beat.)* Whores.

(A silence.)

BEVERLY. Do you enjoy doing this?

ADDIE. Why, of course I do. I look forward to it every year. In fact, if it wasn't Brian's job to put it all together, *I'd* volunteer to do it. I have lots of ideas for tableaus they haven't even tried yet.

BEVERLY. You're just like my son. He's a real idea person too. *(SHE rubs her shoulder.)* I need a massage.

(Without saying a word ADDIE begins to massage BEVERLY's shoulders. BEVERLY first seems surprised by this act of kindness, then almost immediately allows herself to relax into it.)

ADDIE. What happened to Maureen?

BEVERLY. Maureen?

ADDIE. The woman you replaced.

BEVERLY. Brian says it's a cold.

ADDIE. It must be a bad cold. Maureen's never missed a Tableau Weekend.

BEVERLY. Keeping her home was Brian's idea. He didn't want her coughing and sneezing. He said it would ruin the effect.

ADDIE. Oh Lord, that reminds me of the time *I* had a coughing fit. I was supposed to be playing a preacher's wife. I was supposed to pretend like I was singing a hymn to Jesus but I just stood there hacking away like a tuberculosis patient.

BEVERLY. How much longer do we have to do this?

ADDIE. Until five o'clock.

(She stops massaging BEVERLY.)

ADDIE. *(Cont.)* Didn't your son give you the participants' packet?

BEVERLY. No. He just burst into the bedroom, threw these clothes at me, and told me I had five minutes to get dressed and into the car. Oh, thank you for the massage.

ADDIE. You're welcome. Brian didn't even ask if you wanted to do it?

BEVERLY. Of course not. I came for a three-day visit and I'm spending one whole day of it pretending to beat a rug. *(Beat, thinking.)* There is a small silver lining, though. My daughter-in-law and I can use the break from one another. Oh — breaks. Do we get bathroom breaks?

ADDIE. *(Nodding.)* Every two hours you get to pee. They close the gallery and put up a sign that says, "Exhibit temporarily inaccessible."

BEVERLY. It's all very well organized, but that doesn't make it any the less silly.

ADDIE. Silly, but people like it.

BEVERLY. But it really isn't all that relevant to what's going on in the world right now, is it?

ADDIE. It's not about the present. It's about the past. *(Beat.)* It's a taste of yesteryear. Do you still want to switch?

BEVERLY. Are we allowed?

ADDIE. In this case, I think so.

BEVERLY. So when would it *not* be all right?

ADDIE. Well, let's say I was playing a maid and you were playing, like, a very proper uptown lady who I was serving breakfast to. Don't you think it would be strange if all of the sudden the maid is eating off the fine china and the hoity woman is pouring her coffee?

BEVERLY. *(Grinning.)* Oh yes. It would be an absolute scandal! *(ADDIE smiles too.)* Your accent is stronger than the others. Where are you from?

ADDIE. I grew up in the hills. I moved down to the city when I married. *(Showing BEVERLY her teeth.)* I still have all my teeth. Where I come from: that's a major accomplishment. So would you like to change places?

(BEVERLY nods. They start to exchange positions just as a group of four PROMENADERS ENTER: two women, a man, and a little girl. ADDIE and BEVERLY are forced to hold where they are: ADDIE on her way to the rug and BEVERLY moving toward the butter churn. The FOURSOME stop and stare.)

MAN. *(Assessing the tableau.)* They could be dancing.

FIRST WOMAN. That doesn't look like dancing to me.

MAN. *(To the second woman.)* Well, what do *you* think they're doing?

SECOND WOMAN. I don't know, but it looks to me like somebody's up to no good. See how that pharmacist's assistant is touching that other woman?

FIRST WOMAN. For the love of Mike! How are you getting that?

GIRL. Isn't that the same woman who played the old hooker two years ago?

SECOND WOMAN. *(Chastising.)* Vicki, *really!*

MAN. If I had set it up, I would have put one of the women at the butter churn and the other woman over at the rug.

FIRST WOMAN. What's she doing with that broom?

GIRL. I think she's going to swat that hooker with it.

SECOND WOMAN. Vicki, just be quiet.

MAN. I'm not all that fond of this one.

FIRST WOMAN. Me neither. Let's go see the firehouse. *(To Vicki.)* Honey, would you like to see the firemen?

VICKI. I'll bet she's going to use that broom to do a pole dance!

SECOND WOMAN. *(To MAN.)* Marvin, are you letting our daughter watch HBO while I'm on night shift?

MAN. *(Contrite.)* I fall asleep.

(The MAN moves on. The WOMEN and little VICKI follow. After they are gone, ADDIE and BEVERLY break their poses and dissolve into laughter.)

BEVERLY. All right. That was funny.

ADDIE. The comments people make — oh, Beverly, they're simply priceless!

BEVERLY. *(Positioning herself over the churn.)* Is this right?

ADDIE. Well, you might want to put a little more back into it. But, I mean, don't go overboard, honey. This isn't great art here.

(ADDIE takes up the broom.)

ADDIE. *(Cont.)* If you want to know the truth of it: this isn't one of my favorites.

BEVERLY. Oh?

ADDIE. Not because of you. I mean, you're a very nice change after the last five years with Maureen. The only time I can half-way deal with her is when she — *(Conspiratorially.)* Well, she makes these goo-goo eyes at the babies when nobody's looking. It's all I can do to keep from busting out laughing. *(Laughs.)* But what I mean about this particular tableau is that when you stop to think about it, I mean it really isn't very realistic, is it? What woman would beat a rug so close to another person like this? The dust would go flying all over the place. It would be rude and inconsiderate. Don't you think?

BEVERLY. I would think so, yes.

ADDIE. You really should think about coming back next year. I'll ask Brian to team us up. Or, my goodness, you can just ask him yourself. I'm sure we'll get a much better assignment next year.

BEVERLY. It does sound like fun, dear, but I'm afraid I won't be here next year. I really don't get down to see my son very often. He and Debbie usually come up to see *me*. *(Correcting herself.)* Well, *he* does, anyway. I can't remember the last time *she* came up.

ADDIE. Oh. *(Beat.)* Where do you live?

BEVERLY. New York.

ADDIE. City?

BEVERLY. Yes.

ADDIE. Oh. *(Beat.)* Well you're certainly a little ways from home. *(Beat.)* What do you do?

BEVERLY. I'm an interior designer. Corporate work mostly. I do space planning, office design.

ADDIE. Do you enjoy it?

BEVERLY. Sometimes.

ADDIE. Have you ever thought about moving to Dix?

BEVERLY. That probably wouldn't be a very good idea.

ADDIE. Why is that?

BEVERLY. Oh, I'm sure Brian and Debbie prefer me there and them here.

ADDIE. How old are you?

BEVERLY. Well aren't you all about the questions? I just turned sixty-one.

ADDIE. Well, goodness! I did too. When is your birthday?

BEVERLY. May second.

ADDIE. My Lord, Beverly Duggins, I am a mere one week older than you! What an amazing coincidence.

BEVERLY. Yes, the odds would be against that sort of thing wouldn't they?

(A MAN and WOMAN ENTER. ADDIE and BEVERLY stiffen up and train their gazes on points in the distance.)

WOMAN. This isn't right.

MAN. What?

WOMAN. Well, when I was here earlier ... *(Pointing.)* ... she was *there* and she was *there!*

MAN. Are you sure about this?

WOMAN. Yes. They changed places. Statues aren't supposed to rearrange themselves like that.

MAN. What difference does it make?

WOMAN. Well, it's just a little disconcerting, that's all. *(To ADDIE and BEVERLY, accusatory.)* I *know* what you *did!*

(She storms off.)

MAN. *(To ADDIE and BEVERLY, sincerely.)* I'm sorry. She's going into therapy.

(He goes off.)

ADDIE. Good Lord! Did you look at her face!

BEVERLY. This town is full of—

ADDIE. Lunatics! Dix is a lunatic town. Your son has become the director of the Museum of Crazytown.

BEVERLY. But in a, well, *fun* way.

ADDIE. If you want the truth of it — and I know because I see all the prescriptions: most everybody in this town is on some form of medication: Zoloft, Remeron, Sarfem, Wellbutrin, Lexapro, Paxil, Prozac, Celexa, Zoloft.

BEVERLY. You said Zoloft.

ADDIE. Buspirone, Effexor. Did I say Xanax?

BEVERLY. You didn't say Xanax.

ADDIE. Makes you want to laugh and cry at the same time.

BEVERLY. *(With growing, genuine interest.)* It does, doesn't it?

ADDIE. Which is why, I think, getting together once a year to stand around like statues doesn't sound like too unusual a thing to do — at least not here in Dix. *(ADDIE sees something.)* Now what's *she* doing here?

(A woman who we soon learn is the supposedly infirmed MAUREEN flies in, dressed as a frontier wife. SHE looks a little disheveled.)

MAUREEN. I'm so sorry I'm late.

ADDIE. Brian said you were sick.

MAUREEN. I'm fine. I had a little cold but I'm all be— [tter] *(Coughs.)* I ran. I'm out of breath. *(Coughs.)* I'll be all right. *(To BEVERLY.)* Hello. I'm Maureen. You can go now.

(BEVERLY looks puzzled.)

BEVERLY. Go?

(SHE glances at ADDIE.)

MAUREEN. Yes. Thank you for helping out. But I can take it from here. Addie, what are you doing at the rug?

BEVERLY. *(To ADDIE.)* Did I just get replaced?

MAUREEN. You just got replaced. *(She takes the broom from ADDIE. To ADDIE.)* You're supposed to churning butter.

ADDIE. *(handing MAUREEN the broom.)* Beverly's arm was getting tired.

MAUREEN. Well, my arms *never* get tired, do they? *(To BEVERLY.)* I once held a baby doll up in the air for the doctor to spank her little bottom — I held that baby over my head for six full hours, didn't I, Addie?

ADDIE. You did, I remember.

MAUREEN. So thank you very much, Mrs. Duggins. The museum appreciates your service.

(BEVERLY is about to step off the platform; MAUREEN is about to move with the broom to the rug; and ADDIE is about to position herself back at the butter churn, when a MAN and WOMAN ENTER. The TRIO notices the couple and freeze where they are, nearly simultaneously.)

WOMAN. What have we here?

MAN. *(Regarding BEVERLY.)* Well, that one right there: she's heading over to the barn, I betcha. To check on the cows.

WOMAN. The *cows*?

MAN. Yeah. 'See if they need milking.

WOMAN. Oh, that would be a funny little scene, wouldn't it? You know, they ought to bring in some real animals to liven things up. That would be riot, wouldn't it? A real live cow in the museum.

MAN. Now how are they going to get that cow to be perfectly still, LuAnne?

WOMAN. Well, can't they be trained or something? Oh would you look at how she's beating that rug! Looks like she's just jabbing at it. That isn't going to clean a rug! I'd like to see a real cow. I'm going to put that in the suggestion box.

MAN. Are we through here? I want to check out that firehouse.

WOMAN. She's not churning right either. Her hands are hardly even touching the churn stick.

MAN. Fine. Let's go see the firemen. They've got one of those fellows kind of poised right in the middle of a pole slide. I've got to see how they pull that one off.

WOMAN. *(As they start off.)* This one was a real disappointment.

(The COUPLE go off.)

BEVERLY. It's official: we're a disappointment. *(To ADDIE.)* Maybe you can redeem yourselves once I'm gone.

MAUREEN. Why, of course we can! *(She goes into the pose, striking a much more animated stance than BEVERLY or ADDIE did — one, in fact, that hardly looks sustainable for any length of time. To BEVERLY.)* Thank you again for helping out.

ADDIE. *(To BEVERLY, warmly, sincerely.)* Yes. Thank you. I enjoyed getting to know you a little. Your son — he really is doing an excellent job.

BEVERLY. Thank you. *(Almost sadly.)* Well, all right. Goodbye then.

ADDIE. *(Almost sadly herself.)* Goodbye. Have a safe trip back to New York.

(BEVERLY nods. SHE starts to leave in the opposite direction of the couple's EXIT.)

MAUREEN. *(To BEVERLY.)* Don't you want to see the firemen?

BEVERLY. Oh, yes. I should see the firemen.

(SHE turns and goes off the other way. ADDIE watches her EXIT, looking unmistakably disappointed. LIGHTS fade out. In the darkness we hear:)

A YOUNG GIRL'S VOICE. *(Struggling to read something aloud.)* Beauty is no recent phemonoma— phee— phee—

A WOMAN'S VOICE. *(Helpful.)* Phenomenon.

GIRL'S VOICE. *(Continuing.)* The women of the town of Dix have always prided themselves on their appearances from the days of hoop skirts and bustles to the hair bobs and flapper shorty-skirts of the twenties up to the mod fashions of today. In 1931, the Spit and Curl opened on Main Street and has been operating there ever since. An insti— insititu— instu—

A WOMAN'S VOICE. Institution.

GIRL'S VOICE. Institution of the town. Where women have for over seventy years gabbed and gossiped and curled and primped themselves to beautemous —

A WOMAN'S VOICE. Beauteous.

GIRL'S VOICE. What's "beauteous"?

A WOMAN VOICE. It's like beautiful.

GIRL'S VOICE. Oh. Beautemous perfection.

A WOMAN'S VOICE. Good Lord, who writes this stuff?

(LIGHTS come up in the gallery. The WOMAN and GIRL whose voices we apparently just heard stand looking at a tableau of one of the beauty "stations" at the Spit and Curl. BEVERLY is seated in the chair with her hair done up in medusa-like electrified curlers. SHE holds a bottle of Coca-Cola in one hand and a screen magazine in the other. ADDIE, the beauty operator, stands behind her, a fake cigarette dangling from one side of

her mouth.)

GIRL. Look, Mama — she's going to have a real curly head.

WOMAN. She's going to look like a big old lady Shirley Temple, isn't she? *(They laugh. BEVERLY frowns slightly at this disparagement. THE WOMAN turns to the little girl.)* Do you want to see the firemen?

GIRL. We saw the firemen last year.

WOMAN. But there's a lot more of them this year. And they're actually putting out a fire.

GIRL. *(Running out.)* A real fire? Really?

(HER mother follows.)

MOTHER. *(Over her shoulders.)* Nice work, ladies.

(BEVERLY and ADDIE relax, chuckling.)

ADDIE. I hate those firemen. They show us up. Every year. So you were telling me —

BEVERLY. I was already planning to come at the end of the month — to see the baby. I just decided to move it up a little bit.

ADDIE. I'm so glad you did. It was such a pleasant surprise to walk into that room and see you with that cherry turnover in your mouth. Brian hadn't even told me.

BEVERLY. He didn't know until the last minute. *(Beat.)* How is Maureen taking it?

ADDIE. Not too well, I don't think. She was really looking forward to this one. She's never been a beauty parlor customer before.

BEVERLY. Well, when Maureen's son gets to be director of the museum she can have *me* bumped if she likes.

ADDIE. I'm *glad* he bumped her. It serves her right. She's so bossy.

BEVERLY. Where did Brian end up putting her?

ADDIE. *(Nodding.)* In the Yellow Fever ward. She says she hates it there. She says they've got her in a back bed where you can hardly even see her. And it isn't even a full-sized bed. She has to pull her legs up to her chest and pretend to be a sick child. She isn't very happy.

BEVERLY. *(Trying desperately to be sympathetic but tickled in spite of herself.)* That's terrible!

(ADDIE has lost all self-control herself; she bursts out laughing.)

ADDIE. Oh, it's awful!

BEVERLY. It appears that my son is working on a slightly grander scale this year.

ADDIE. He is so good, Beverly. He is so much better than Mr. Creel.

BEVERLY. And how long was Mr. Creel here?

ADDIE. Oh good Lord. Over forty years, I know that. And, of course, he ran out of fresh ideas along about year two! The worst thing of all was that he'd never listen to anybody else's ideas. One year, for example, I suggested that maybe we should have a hoe-down tableau. A real old fashioned knee-slapping hoe down. Well, he just killed that one right in the crib. He said it would give people leg cramps having to hold their legs in funny ways like that. Then he went and lost his mind and everything became — what's the word?

BEVERLY. Moot?

ADDIE. Yes. It all became moot.

BEVERLY. He lost his —

ADDIE. It wasn't like Alzheimers or anything. It was just like one morning he woke up and there he was — sitting on the edge of his bed, mentally insane. I understand he came to the museum with Pepsodent all gunking up his beard and started cutting little dime size holes in the museum's only Grandma Moses. Do you know how much we had to pay to get that painting, and now it isn't worth jack!

BEVERLY. I can imagine.

ADDIE. Oh, it was such a delightful winter scene. Now it's got all these holes in it you could put your finger through. Do you like art?

BEVERLY. Yes I do. Very much.

ADDIE. I'm here every week. Did I tell you I'm a volunteer? I take school children through the museum. That's what I was doing the morning Mr. Creel vandalized that Grandma Moses painting. And then if that wasn't enough, those poor kids had to watch that insane man go over to that Madonna and Child and aim those scissors right at the Virgin Mary's suckle breast. He came this close to cutting out a nipple right there in front of all those impressionable little children and that hungry baby Jesus. But luckily somebody knocked that madman to the floor before he could do any more damage. *(Beat.)* I love art.

BEVERLY. Have you ever been to New York?

ADDIE. I never have.

BEVERLY. We have some wonderful art museums.

ADDIE. Oh yes, I know. That's where you've got some of those beautiful Vermers. I love Vermer. You learn things from Vermer. You learn that those Dutch people liked to look out windows. *(BEVERLY tries to hide a smile. ADDIE looks about.)* Where is everybody?

BEVERLY. I think they're looking at the firemen and the Yellow Fever victims.

ADDIE. That's fine. It gives us some time to catch up. Did you have a good year?

BEVERLY. *(Smiling.)* I just became a grandmother.

ADDIE. That's right! That's right! And how does it feel?

BEVERLY. Like it was about time. Brian and Debbie waited fifteen years to have their first baby.

ADDIE. You thought it was never going to happen, didn't you?

BEVERLY. They'd always said they didn't want children. It was such a wonderful surprise. Addie, are you —

ADDIE. I'm not married. I used to be married. Many years ago. Long time ago. Somebody's coming.

(A MAN and TWO WOMEN ENTER.)

FIRST WOMAN. Oh look — I like this one! She's getting all fixed up. She's going somewhere special.

MAN. What's with that cigarette?

SECOND WOMAN. People smoked a lot more in olden days. They didn't know the dangers of smoking.

MAN. No. I mean that cigarette looks like a joint.

SECOND WOMAN. Oh, Herbert! It does not!

FIRST WOMAN. You know, I think it *does!* All smushed down like that — that's exactly what it looks like!

SECOND WOMAN. Well, if that's the case, I'm not quite sure I know what they're trying to say here.

MAN. *(Playfully.)* That beauty parlors in Dix used to be hot little dens of iniquity.

SECOND WOMAN. You two are terrible! How are you going to face Addie in church tomorrow, after all this talk?

MAN. Addie knows we're just having fun. *(HE winks at ADDIE who has a hard time suppressing a grin.)* But it *does* look like weed, Addie. I'd do something about that if I was you.

(The THREE EXIT. ADDIE removes the cigarette from her mouth and examines it.)

ADDIE. *(To Beverly.)* Does this look like weed to you?

BEVERLY. Well... yes.

ADDIE. You try holding a cigarette in your mouth all morning and see if it doesn't stop looking like a real cigarette after a while.

BEVERLY. Why don't you get a fresh one?

ADDIE. It's all I have. I don't smoke.

BEVERLY. Here. *(Reaching under the bib-sheet.)* Have one of mine.

ADDIE. You smoke?

BEVERLY. As of about three months ago.

ADDIE. Oh Lord, Beverly — you're kidding me. *(BEVERLY produces a cigarette pack and taps one out for ADDIE.)* Now why would you go and do something like that?

BEVERLY. Stress — who knows? They cut back my hours. The architectural firm where I work. It isn't doing well. The whole industry's taken a hit. I have time on my hands now, Addie, and I have all this nervous energy.

ADDIE. So what are you doing when you're not working?

BEVERLY. Wishing I were working.

ADDIE. Maybe you should just enjoy the rest. Maybe you should go right ahead and retire and start a brand new chapter of your life.

BEVERLY. I'm not ready to retire. *(With a pregnancy of meaning that will later be revealed.)* And I need the insurance.

ADDIE. You could do volunteer work.

BEVERLY. Yes, I'm thinking about it. You're inspiring me, Addie.

ADDIE. I am?

BEVERLY. Oh yes.

ADDIE. Well, that was — that was a very sweet—

BEVERLY. Do you like working at the drug store?

ADDIE. Some days I wish I was doing something else. But mostly it's not a bad place to be. And I like helping people. *(THEY both smile. Long beat.)* Did you really come two weeks early just to do this tableau? *(BEVERLY nods: a revelation.)* Why?

BEVERLY. I had a good time last year.

ADDIE. We make a good team, don't you think?

BEVERLY. We do. *(Beat.)* I was think—

(SHE stops herself.)

ADDIE. *(Curious.)* What? What were you thinking about, Beverly Duggins?

BEVERLY. Oh, it's so silly.

ADDIE. Please.

BEVERLY. I was thinking that over the past year — there were a few times I came very close to calling you.

ADDIE. You did? Really? *(BEVERLY nods.)* But you didn't.

BEVERLY. No. I — didn't have your number.

ADDIE. I'm not listed. It's kind of stupid. It's not a very big city. Everybody knows me. But I was getting these — well — *(A whisper.)* — obscene phone calls. So I changed my number to an unlisted one.

BEVERLY. You could have reported those calls, you know.

ADDIE. Well, the thing is: I knew who it was. My brother. He isn't well. He calls me from Needles, California and says things that just aren't very nice, and now I have an unlisted number and he can't say those things anymore.

BEVERLY. He doesn't come here in person to bother you?

ADDIE. No. He's in an iron lung. Travel is an inconvenience for him.

BEVERLY. He calls you up from the iron lung and harasses you?

ADDIE. Yes.

BEVERLY. But someone would have to — well, dial for him, right?

ADDIE. Lana. His nurse. Lana dials and then she holds the phone up to his mouth so he can say all those nasty things and then he has her hang up.

BEVERLY. She goes along with this?

ADDIE. Apparently, yes. *(Beat.)* One time she even joined in.

BEVERLY. That's all a little sick, Addie.

ADDIE. A *little?* I excuse him because he's disturbed. This is what I've been trying to tell you: my world is full of screwy people. You, Beverly Duggins, are a blessing and a joy.

BEVERLY. But you *must* have other family.

ADDIE. Just a couple of first cousins who live on a boat somewhere, but it's hard to count them. I mean, they don't ever come ashore except to buy groceries and go to the dentist. *(Beat.)* I had a son. *(Beat.)* I had a husband and a son. *(Beat.)* I used to have a family. *(Beat.)* You really thought about calling me? You should have called me. Brian has my number. *(Beat, then softly.)* You should have called me.

BEVERLY. Yes. I know.

(BEVERLY'S hand reaches up and finds ADDIE's. They hold like this. A moment passes. Suddenly, TWO WOMEN ENTER. BEVERLY and ADDIE are forced to freeze in this position.)

FIRST WOMAN. *(Taking in the tableau.)* Hmmmm.

(FAST FADE TO BLACK. In the DARKNESS we hear a man's voice.)

A MAN'S VOICE. *(As if reading.)* Parker's Dairy has been a Dix mainstay for the last one-hundred-and-twenty-years.

WOMAN'S VOICE. They used to deliver.

MAN'S VOICE. Remember that little slip you'd fill out for the milkman the night before? Like if you needed butter or cream?

WOMAN'S VOICE. Cream! Good Lord! Remember when people drank cream? I used to put it on my cereal. On my corn flakes. Now I drink skim and still I look like a cow.

MAN'S VOICE. You do not.

WOMAN'S VOICE. Of course I do. I look just like that cow right there.

(LIGHTS come up on this tableau: A life-size papier-machè jersey cow is being milked by ADDIE who sits on a little wooden milking stool and wears period (perhaps turn-of-the-20th Century) farm clothes. BEVERLY has been captured in the act of carrying over a milk pail. A MAN and WOMAN, the presumed source of the voices we just heard, stand admiring the tableau.)

MAN. That's one helluva cow.

WOMAN. I think one of the teats fell off.

MAN. Really? Where?

WOMAN. By her foot.

MAN. Well, it's still a great tableau. *(To ADDIE and BEVERLY.)* Very Currier and Ives, ladies. A real treat. *(To the WOMAN.)* Let's go see the marching band.

WOMAN. All right.

(THE COUPLE EXIT. ADDIE begins to look around her feet. BEVERLY sets down her pail and moves over to ADDIE.)

ADDIE. I don't see it.

BEVERLY. *(Pointing.)* There it is. Right there.
ADDIE. I'll be darned. Bessie lost a teat.
BEVERLY. Can you put it back on?
ADDIE. I'm not sure.

(SHE picks up the detached teat and tries to push it back into the udder.)

BEVERLY. Maybe if we had some glue.
ADDIE. It's already kind of sticky. Maybe if I just pushed it really hard... *(Which she does.)* ... and just held it there for a moment.

(A WOMAN and YOUNG GIRL ENTER. ADDIE and BEVERLY must freeze their positions.)

WOMAN. And look. Here's an old dairy barn.
GIRL. What's the lady doing?
WOMAN. She's milking the cow. See? She's sitting on the stool and the other lady is going over to see how much milk she's gotten.
GIRL. Why is she pushing on the cow's tummy like that?
WOMAN. It's probably a special way to milk. She's massaging the cow, I guess, to get the milk to flow.
GIRL. Can I taste some milk?
WOMAN. No you may not. It probably isn't even real milk.
GIRL. It's not a real cow either. Uh oh. I think one of those little pull-down things just fell off.
WOMAN. Well, let's go on, dear, and let these milkmaids get that poor cow to the vet.

(They go out.)

BEVERLY. *(To ADDIE, pointing.)* By your other foot. Bessie seems to be dropping her little tits all over the place this morning.

ADDIE. *(Pulling her hand away.)* It's hopeless. This cow's going to put the Parker Dairy out of business. *(BEVERLY begins to massage her leg. ADDIE notices.)* What's wrong with your leg?

BEVERLY. I banged my knee at the airport. On somebody's trunk. I didn't know people still traveled with trunks.

ADDIE. My husband did. Do you want me to look at it?

BEVERLY. Oh, it's probably all ugly black and blue. I'd rather you not.

ADDIE. At least sit down.

(SHE offers the milking stool to BEVERLY, who slowly eases down onto it. It sits very low to the ground and SHE looks a little comical upon it. ADDIE giggles.)

BEVERLY. Now that's exactly what my husband would have done.

ADDIE. What?

BEVERLY. Put me in a silly spot and then step back and laugh at me.

ADDIE. And this a good thing or a bad thing?

BEVERLY. Well, I'd have to say when *he* did it, it was almost endearing.

ADDIE. What was your husband's name?

BEVERLY. Kevin. We had eighteen great years before he died. An aneurysm took him.

ADDIE. He was a lawyer, I think Brian told me.

BEVERLY. *(Nodding.)* Kevin had a small store-front office. 'Hardly made a dime. But we were happy. And he gave me Brian. Once — right after we got married — it would be years before he'd be able to top this one — we were at the supermarket together —

newlyweds at the supermarket, we were so cute together, Addie, it would have made you want to vomit — we're standing in the check-out line, and I've got my head in a magazine and he sneaks off and when he comes back a little bit later he's got this huge — this absolute *mammoth*-sized wheel of cheddar cheese — which he proceeds to place right into our shopping cart. It was from a display, Addie. You could have used it for a coffee table! And if that wasn't bad enough, he *leaves!* He goes running off like a giggly Halloween prankster, and I'm left with this gigantic display wheel of cheese and it's far too heavy for me to pull out myself and by this point it's my turn with the check-out girl and I have to explain what in God's name this enormous *food product* is doing in my cart and now everyone's laughing at me except for the check-out girl who doesn't see any humor in this at all. I probably would have killed him, Addie, if I didn't love him so much. *(The memory tickles her; she starts laughing.)* I got back at him, though.

ADDIE. What'd you do?

BEVERLY. I bought it.

ADDIE. The whole wheel?

BEVERLY. The whole wheel. I wrote out a check. It bounced, of course, and I had to go to work as a nursery school helper for a couple of weeks to cover it. That was before I decided to go back to school and get a degree in interior design.

ADDIE. And did you and Kevin eat all that cheese?

BEVERLY. Oh, goodness no. We gave most of it away to the local soup kitchens.

(ADDIE joins BEVERLY in laughter.)

BEVERLY. What did *your* husband do for a living?

ADDIE. Carl was a traveling salesman. He had one trunk for his samples. He had another one for his dummy. Carl was also an amateur ventriloquist.

BEVERLY. Was he any good?

ADDIE. Oh, he was *very* good. I just didn't care for that dummy of his. He was one of those scary dummies that you would sometimes see on the television. He used to frighten Owen like you wouldn't believe.

BEVERLY. Owen was your son?

ADDIE. Yes. And Carl, bless his heart, he did the best he could to keep that dummy from looking so scary. One time he put a pig snout on it, but all that did was make it look like one of those pig doctors in that *Twilight Zone* episode where Ellie May Clampett wakes up and finds out that all of her critters have turned into pig-nosed hospital personnel.

BEVERLY. Addie, dear, half the time I don't know what in the world you're talking about.

ADDIE. *(After a long beat.)* I gave the dummy to the Goodwill.

BEVERLY. How did Carl take losing his dummy like that?

ADDIE. He wasn't very happy. Then a week later none of it made any difference. A week later a drunk truck driver sent my husband and son into the arms of Jesus.

BEVERLY. Oh Addie, I am so sorry.

(ADDIE nods plaintively, apparently hijacked by the memory. She sits down next to BEVERLY. SHE pulls her legs up Indian-style. BEVERLY pivots a bit to face her.)

ADDIE. *(Trying to get a grip on herself.)* Tell me — tell me about the baby.

BEVERLY. Oh, the baby is just fine.

ADDIE. Who does he look like?

BEVERLY. You haven't seen him?

(SHE pulls out her pocket book.)

ADDIE. *(Shaking her head.)* I keep missing him. *(BEVERLY shows her a picture.)* Oh Lord! It's the Gerber baby.

BEVERLY. That's what I think too. Those plump little cheeks. Brian and Debbie want to put him in commercials.

ADDIE. He really is adorable.

BEVERLY. *(Putting the pocket book away.)* Now I'm sure Brian wouldn't have minded at all if you'd dropped by the house.

ADDIE. I don't know — I didn't want to impose...

BEVERLY. That's just silly. And you could certainly have called first if you'd thought it was a bad time.

ADDIE. Yes, I could have. *(Intending more here than the obvious.)* Because I don't have a problem with the phone.

BEVERLY. *(Apparently understanding why ADDIE said this.)* Oh. *(Beat.)* Well. You know what? Addie, I am just not good about staying in touch with people, that's all.

ADDIE. Last year you said that you'd thought about calling me.

BEVERLY. I did. You're right.

(An awkward silence.)

ADDIE. And you got the two messages I left?

BEVERLY. Yes, I did.

ADDIE. I don't understand. We seem to get along so well when you come down. We have such a good time.

BEVERLY. *(Nodding.)* We do. A lovely time.

ADDIE. And I thought we had become friends.

(BEVERLY seems to want to say something. A MAN ENTERS with TWO WOMEN and a GIRL. They all stop and study the tableau

for a moment.)

FIRST WOMAN. *(Assessing.)* They're taking a break.

MAN. That cow could kick her in the head.

GIRL. Look. That moo-cow's boosies have all fallen off.

SECOND WOMAN. Let's go see the marching band.

(They all EXIT.)

BEVERLY. They *have* all fallen off, haven't they? Every single one of them. *(Beat.)* I know a little something about that.

ADDIE. *(After taking a moment to process.)* When?

BEVERLY. The surgery was last June.

ADDIE. Did you know — last year when you were here?

BEVERLY. Yes.

ADDIE. But you didn't say anything.

BEVERLY. No. *(Beat.)* That isn't me, Addie. I don't do that.

ADDIE. Just tell me that you didn't go through it alone.

BEVERLY. My son was there. And before and after he was always a phone call away.

ADDIE. What about all your girlfriends in New York?

BEVERLY. I don't have "girlfriends," Addie.

ADDIE. You have friends, I'm sure.

BEVERLY. If you want to know the hard truth, Addie — I'm not a big collector of friends. There are a few people I work with. I'm on good terms with them. And I have my son. And now I have my new grandson. I don't have much need for all that many people in my life.

ADDIE. Don't need them or don't want them?

BEVERLY. I keep my own company quite well, Addie. I always have. And I happen to have, well, for want of any other way to put this — I have high *standards*. For friendship. I know that must sound so arrogant, but that's who I am. Will you help me up?

(ADDIE helps BEVERLY to her feet.)

ADDIE. What if you just need to talk?

BEVERLY. The feeling usually passes. Or I talk to my son for a few minutes. Hearing his voice is always a comfort. *(Beat.)* Addie, I am just not a very socially oriented person. I never have been.

ADDIE. Me neither. I try to be, but... *(BEVERLY looks at her a little suspiciously.)* No. I'm not just saying that. I see a lot of people — here, at work, at my church. But I don't have *close* friends either. For whatever reason. Maybe I'm too busy — maybe I'm too busy to give myself over to another person for whatever reason.

BEVERLY. *(Chuckles.)* I don't have friends because I think I'm too good for everybody. You don't have friends because you're too damned busy. Well, I suppose one might think these are viable reasons for our present situations, right?

(SHE takes a step and winces.)

ADDIE. Don't you think you should have that x-rayed?

BEVERLY. Not until after five o'clock. We've done such a good job of marginalizing Maureen up to now.

(She picks up her pail. ADDIE sits down on the stool and turns to the cow.)

ADDIE. But at least tell me this: when we get together, Beverly. Once a year — we have a good time.

BEVERLY. We have a wonderful time, Addie. At least when my leg isn't banged up.

ADDIE. So the rest of the year doesn't matter.

BEVERLY. No. It shouldn't matter at all.

ADDIE. *(indicating BEVERLY's breast by touching her own.)* What's the prognosis?

BEVERLY. The prognosis is very good. The doctor was very encouraged. I just have one less tit.

ADDIE. Lord.

BEVERLY. Do friends — are friends allowed to say things like that?

ADDIE. Friends can say whatever they please.

(A MAN and WOMAN ENTER. As they move to the tableau, LIGHTS fade out. In the darkness, we hear ADDIE and BEVERLY'S VOICES, altered to sound as if they are filtered through a telephone microphone.)

BEVERLY'S VOICE. Addie?

ADDIE'S VOICE. Yes?

BEVERLY'S VOICE. It's Beverly.

ADDIE'S VOICE. Oh my goodness, honey. I didn't recognize your voice on the phone.

BEVERLY'S VOICE. How are you?

ADDIE'S VOICE. I'm fine. How are *you*?

BEVERLY'S VOICE. I'm doing well.

ADDIE'S VOICE. I can't believe you called.

BEVERLY'S VOICE. Addie, I can't make it down to Dix next week.

ADDIE'S VOICE. Oh. Is everything all right?

BEVERLY'S VOICE. Something's come up.

ADDIE'S VOICE. Oh. *(Beat.)* All right.

BEVERLY'S VOICE. Something I can't get out of. I'm really sorry. I didn't want you to wonder where I was.

ADDIE'S VOICE. Thank you for letting me know.

BEVERLY'S VOICE. I thought you'd want to know.

ADDIE'S VOICE. Yes. Thank you. *(Beat.)* Well.

BEVERLY'S VOICE. Yes. Well, I'll let you go.

ADDIE'S VOICE. I'm glad you called.

BEVERLY'S VOICE. Take care of yourself. Say hello to Maureen for me.

ADDIE'S VOICE. Yes. All right.

BEVERLY'S VOICE. Goodbye, Addie.

ADDIE'S VOICE. Goodbye, Beverly.

(LIGHTS come up dimly on a large contemporary-styled arm chair. The light source is an unseen window. The last rays of twilight cast long shadows over the chair and its OCCUPANT who sits in the semi-darkness holding an open magazine limply in her lap. LIGHTS come up slowly, almost imperceptibly, to reveal a gaze fixed on nothing in particular, a look of emotional detachment, and finally, the clear identity of the occupant. It is BEVERLY. SHE sits silent, still. SHE has become an inadvertent tableau. SHE is "the lonely woman in a chair." LIGHTS fade out. In the total darkness, we hear a MAN and a WOMAN speaking.)

WOMAN'S VOICE. Is it night school?

MAN'S VOICE. If it was night school, it would be dark. Does it look dark to you?

WOMAN'S VOICE. But she looks much too old to still be in school.

MAN'S VOICE. It could be college. It could be she's in college.

WOMAN'S VOICE. She looks too old for college too. She looks fifty if she's a day.

MAN'S VOICE. She turned around. I didn't think that they were supposed to move.

(Now we hear a different WOMAN'S VOICE.)

SECOND VOICE. Why don't you go on now — the both of you — and mind your own business!

(LIGHTS snap on. We now realize that the second voice belongs to MAUREEN who is turned around in her student's desk in a mock-up of a high school classroom. Instead of facing forward and upstage to look at ADDIE who stands with pointer in hand before a chalk board, SHE is glaring at the male and female promenaders who stand slightly cowering a few feet away. MAUREEN is dressed as a parody of a 1950s teenager. ADDIE wears the attire of the prim school teacher, complete with hair pinned up into a bun and June Cleaver pearls.)

MAUREEN.. You heard me! Scat!

MAN. *(To MAUREEN.)* You're not supposed to talk either!

MAUREEN. *(To the MAN.)* Well, I can't help myself. I have never been so insulted in my life.

WOMAN. *(Contrite.)* I didn't think you could hear me.

MAN. Maureen, we didn't even know it was you. All we could see was the back of your head, we swear.

MAUREEN. *(To the man.)* I don't care. You shouldn't talk that way about *anybody*. I have a mind to ask Howard to pull his account from your bank.

MAN. Maureen, honey, you don't want to do that.

WOMAN. Of course she doesn't. She's going to forget this even happened. And tomorrow, why, I'm going to bring over a bundt cake, and everything will be right back to normal, won't it?

(MAUREEN doesn't answer. She turns back around in her seat so she now faces ADDIE upstage.)

MAN. *(To the woman.)* Come on Margaret — we're just making it worse.

WOMAN. I really *am* sorry, Maureen.

(The COUPLE starts off.)

MAUREEN. Pound cake.

(The COUPLE stops.)

WOMAN. What was that?

MAUREEN. Pound cake. Not bundt cake.

MAN. Good. You got it. Let's go, Margaret.

(The COUPLE EXITS.)

MAUREEN. *(To ADDIE.)* Now how do you like that! The nerve! The absolute nerve!

ADDIE. Maybe they honestly didn't know it was you. I mean sometimes it *is* hard to tell who a person is from the back of their head.

MAUREEN. Maybe they didn't know it was me, but that was still a very rude thing to say. *(Beat.)* Does Brian hate me?

ADDIE. Now why would you ask that?

MAUREEN. Because he's got me sitting so that nobody can even see my face. It's like the year Mr. Creel asked me to be a bee keeper. I never even got to take off the hood. I was burning up in that outfit and if I hadn't stitched my name over the pocket, nobody would have even known it was me.

ADDIE. What if I was to come stand about right here — *(Goes to Maureen.)* — and you scoot out a little bit and I lean over like I'm helping you with your school work?

MAUREEN. Well, they're still not going to be able to see my face because you'd still be blocking me. I really honestly think that Brian has it in for me, I do. I'm just about ready to stop doing these tableaus.

ADDIE. Maybe I could talk to him.

MAUREEN. Or better yet: talk to his mother. She could put in a good word for me, don't you think? *(Beat.)* Where is she?

ADDIE. I don't think she's here, Maureen.

MAUREEN. Come to think of it, I don't remember seeing her last year either.

ADDIE. I think she's stopped coming. I have an idea: I could sit in your desk and you stand right here next to me.

MAUREEN. But that wouldn't make any sense. Why would the teacher be seated and the pupil be the one standing?

ADDIE. Maybe I'm writing you a hall pass and you're about to go fetch something for me from the principal's office.

MAUREEN. Now how would anybody know that was what was happening?

ADDIE. *(Suddenly snapping, angrily.)* WELL, YOU COULD TURN THE HELL AROUND AND TELL THEM, NOW COULDN'T YOU?

(The shock of ADDIE's outburst silences MAUREEN for a moment, but she quickly regains her voice.)

MAUREEN. I'm sorry, Addie. It just really bothered me that Margaret would have said such a snide thing like that.

ADDIE. Maureen, you're fifty-three! Fifty would be a compliment, would it not!

MAUREEN. I don't look anything near fifty and you know it. *(Beat.)* And pardon me for saying it, but you have been in a very bad mood since we got here.

ADDIE. To tell you the truth, I don't like doing these things anymore, either.

MAUREEN. Well, *that's* something I never thought I'd hear you say.

ADDIE. They're silly and old fashioned and they aren't relevant at all to what's going on right now.

MAUREEN. And what's going on in the world right now that we have to put it into this museum of — of *antiquity!*

ADDIE. I guess mostly, Maureen, I've just gotten tired. After thirty-seven years, I'm certainly entitled. After thirty-seven years of coming here and dressing up in scratchy moth-ball-smelling clothes and standing and squatting and bending over until my joints ache, and yet I do it — every year — without fail. Even the year of the car crash. Even the year my husband and son got snatched away from me like somebody ripping out my soul, Maureen, I dragged myself over here and I pretended to be taking bread out of an oven for seven-and-half-hours, not counting the bathroom breaks in which I stood in front of a mirror and cried until I threw up. And in all those years it never once came to me how really stupid and meaningless all of it was. Because somehow I thought it ought to be good for me. That it might take my mind off the pain. That knot of pain that gets shaved down just a little bit each year, but in the end it never really goes away, Maureen — not really. And standing in one place all day not talking just gives you lots of time to think. To be reminded of what isn't there anymore. And you know what? There's a lot that isn't here. And I'm very tired. And it's time to stop. So I quit. *(Hands her the pointer.)* Here. You can be the teacher. *(Starts off.)* I'm not playing anymore.

MAUREEN. But I'm not dressed to be the teacher! And — and

— where are my students? I can't just stand here all lonely and forlorn. That kind of tableau wouldn't make any sense! Addie, you come back here.

(ADDIE is gone. LIGHTS come up on what appears to be the tableau setting for either a shoe store or the shoe department of a large department store, circa early 1940s. No one is around. A moment passes. BEVERLY enters dressed in a tailored professional woman's outfit of the period. She sits down in one of the customer chairs, pulls out her cell phone and punches in a number.)

BEVERLY. Brian. ... This will just take a min —. ... All right. *(SHE has apparently been asked to hold by her son. SHE waits. SHE gets up and begins to pace. Brian comes back on the line.)* Brian, I got here early because I thought we'd have the chance to talk. ... No. ... No, Brian, that just won't do. Debbie has made it very clear that —... Brian, do you think I *wanted* to get a room at that hotel?... She's made herself perfectly clear: she doesn't want me there. ... Brian, dear, I flew all the way down here to see you — because I am very troubled over where things are headed. ... My relationship with you, for one thing. Access to my grand—... So, those are terms? ... I'm asking you, Brian: are those the terms? ... And you see nothing wrong with — ... I am not making you — no I am certainly not asking you to make that choice. What I am *asking*, if you'd only just listen to me for just a — ... Yes, I know that this is a bad — ... So when *do* we get to talk about this? ... And what am I supposed to do in the meantime? ... So I have to sit here all day long and smell some strange woman's foot and worry over whether I have just lost both my son and my grandson simply because you're shortha— ... That's a silly — ... Well, if you want the God's honest truth, I would rather play the saleswoman, that's why. I had to play the customer in the beauty parlor, and frankly, I am tired of always being on the receiving end of things. ... Brian, I am very close to walking right out of all of your lives right now. *(Looking around her.)* And I cannot believe that in the middle of all this *mess*, you would ask me to do this stupid — ... All right, then. Go. Maybe I'll be here at five. Or maybe I'll be on a plane back to New York.

(She snaps the phone shut. She sits down, fuming. She gets up and starts pacing again, still fuming. Her back is turned as ADDIE ENTERS. ADDIE stops in her tracks. BEVERLY turns. The two WOMEN regard one another uncertainly, neither speaking. ADDIE crosses to the tableau setting. She wears a dress from the early forties. The shoulder pads are exaggerated. She looks somewhat like a female linebacker.)

BEVERLY. *(With calculated formality.)* Are you my customer?

ADDIE. *(Also with formality.)* That depends. Are you going to sell me shoes?

BEVERLY. I'm supposed to sell *somebody* shoes.

ADDIE. Then I guess I'm your customer. *(Beat.)* So which shoes are you going to sell me? Can I pick them out?

(BEVERLY gestures to a stack of shoe boxes. ADDIE goes to boxes and begins to open them. She discovers very quickly that they are all empty.)

ADDIE. There are no shoes in these boxes.

BEVERLY. *(Lost in thought.)* What?

ADDIE. I said, these shoe boxes: they're all empty.

BEVERLY. Oh. *(Beat.)* I suppose that putting shoes in all those boxes would be going for a much higher level of verisimilitude than the usual, wouldn't it?

ADDIE. Vera-what?

BEVERLY. Never mind. Why don't you pick out a pair from the ones on the display rack?

(ADDIE and BEVERLY go to the shoe display. ADDIE looks them over.)

ADDIE. I don't like any of these. *(Picking one up.)* I like this one. Where's the other one?

BEVERLY. It isn't there?

ADDIE. No.

BEVERLY. Someone brought in just one shoe?

ADDIE. Probably someone with just one leg. *(BEVERLY stares at ADDIE, unsmiling.)* Well, why don't you pretend to be trying this one on me and we'll just put lots of tissue in the box so no one needs to know that there isn't a mate.

BEVERLY. That sounds like a good plan. *(ADDIE starts to prepare things for the tableau.)* Maureen said that you walked out last year.

ADDIE. I did.

BEVERLY. She said you left her alone in the classroom. She said it made no narrative sense. People found it troubling.

ADDIE.Maureen was rubbing my nerves raw. I had to get out.

BEVERLY. She said she didn't think you were coming back this year. And then you showed up this morning and stole her apple turnover.

ADDIE. *(Indignant.)* I *did not* steal her turnover! Her hand was on the bear claw so I thought the turnover was available.

BEVERLY. The point —

ADDIE. The point is that I came back. I changed my mind. You changed your mind too, I see. I thought I was never going to see you again... *(With a sarcastic bite.)* ... and wonder of wonders here you are. *(Beat.)* So why are *you* here?

BEVERLY. Brian asked me.

ADDIE. I mean, why are you here in Dix?

BEVERLY. It doesn't matter. The fact is that I'm here, so let's just do this and get it over with.

(A silence. ADDIE sits down.)

ADDIE. Do you want me to pull my chair around a little bit, so people can see both of our faces?

BEVERLY. I couldn't care less if people don't see my face.

ADDIE. I understand.

BEVERLY. What do you mean you understand?

ADDIE. I mean your eyes are red. Either you've gotten a big fat allergy to this museum or you've been crying. I would guess you've been crying. You don't have to tell me why. You don't have to tell me why you didn't come to do the tableaus the last two years. Beverly, you absolutely do not have to tell me a blessed thing. That's the wonderful thing about doing a tableau. You don't have to say a word if you don't want to. *(We hear a BELL ring twice.)* That's the two-minute warning.

BEVERLY. Yes, I know. The two-minute warning was my son's idea.

ADDIE. Was it also your son's idea to do that ridiculous helicopter crash in the north gallery?

BEVERLY. Yes. *(Beat.)* You think it's ridiculous?

ADDIE. Yes. It's like something out of a bad movie.

BEVERLY. I find it very impressive. It's probably the most exciting tableau I've seen here.

ADDIE. But it's based on something that didn't even happen.

BEVERLY. What do you mean?

ADDIE. I mean it's totally made up. Brian is starting to do tableaus of things that never happened. Marilyn Monroe. Marilyn Monroe never came to Dix. Why is Marilyn Monroe sticking her hands in cement here in this museum, I ask you.

BEVERLY. I don't know. *(Beat.)* But I would beg to differ with you about the helicopter crash.

ADDIE. There *was no* crash! It was just a rough landing. A traffic reporter bruised his knee or something. Beverly, there are people in that room over there who have no arms and legs.

BEVERLY. Well, whether it happened that way or not, it's still bringing people into the museum, and that can't be a bad thing.

ADDIE. No. But I think we have to stop calling it the Dix Tableaux. Because that helicopter and all those chopped up people and that Marilyn Monroe-looking woman with cement all over her hands and — and *this* — I'm telling you, Beverly — it's all lies. About this town. Big lies, little lies — it's all the same.

BEVERLY. What do you mean: "and this"?

ADDIE. There were never any lady shoe sellers in Dix back in the olden days. They were all men. Every last one of them. So why are you — a woman — selling me shoes, I wonder?

BEVERLY. I don't know. Can it really be all that important?

ADDIE. The past is important, Beverly. We have to live every day with what — what happened in the past. With — consequences.

BEVERLY. *(Soberly.)* Yes, I know that, Addie.

ADDIE. And besides — *(She takes a moment to marshal her thoughts.)* Everyone is going to the special tableaus. They aren't coming to the traditional ones. No one wants to look at someone trying on a shoe when they can see a chopped-off leg lying next to a flaming helicopter.

BEVERLY. Well, we'll just see if that's true.

(BEVERLY pulls her slanted shoe-fitting stool over next to ADDIE and sits down.)

ADDIE. I'll bet that's a lot more comfortable than the milking stool was.

BEVERLY. You're right. Put your foot up here.. *(ADDIE places her stockinged foot on the slant. A second BELL rings. The two WOMEN freeze. They remain like this for a ridiculously long period of time with no one coming in. Finally, Beverly straightens up.)* Where is everybody? *(ADDIE shoots her an "I told you so" look. SHE gets up and crosses to the boxes of shoes. She picks up several boxes and brings them over.)* What are you doing?

ADDIE. I thought it would be a funny touch if it looked like I was having a lot of trouble making up my mind.

BEVERLY. I like that idea. We could make it look like a New Yorker cartoon.

ADDIE. Beverly, honey, I just decided something. I just decided that I'm not going to let you off the hook. You're going to tell me exactly what happened and I'm not letting up until I get the whole story.

BEVERLY. I don't know what you mean.

ADDIE. Two years ago you called me up on the phone and you said you couldn't come to the Dix Tableaus. I thought it was just for that year. But it wasn't. All this time I've been waiting for an explanation. Was it the cancer? Have you been in the hospital, Beverly? *(BEVERLY shakes her head.)* And why do you show up now?

BEVERLY. Why are you asking so many questions?

(ADDIE doesn't respond. She stares hard at Beverly.)

BEVERLY. Do you want me to admit that I missed you, Addie? I missed you. There. So why are *you* here?

ADDIE. I was wondering if you might be here. I was wondering if this might be the year you came back.

(BEVERLY smiles.)

BEVERLY. Addie, the reason I haven't done the tableaux the last two years is because I haven't been to Dix in the last two years. But I finally decided that I wasn't going to let this thing with Debbie keep me from my son and grandson. I was ready for some kind of resolution.

ADDIE. Debbie. *(Makes a face.)* Last fall she tried to get me fired. Did Brian tell you? I gave her the wrong prescription. I gave her Mr. Duncan's Propecia.

BEVERLY. She didn't check the bag before she left the store?

ADDIE. No. She waited — oh, I don't know — maybe *five* whole hours! And then she called me at home. She called me up and yelled at me right in the middle of *Law and Order.*

BEVERLY. What?

ADDIE. What?

BEVERLY. Which *Law and Order*?

ADDIE. The one with seminal fluids. Anyway, the point of the story is that she is a hateful woman. I know I should be respectful since she's your kin, but I have to speak honestly, Beverly: your daughter-in-law is as mean as a crippled pimp.

BEVERLY. *(Distracted.)* Why does your foot smell so nice?

ADDIE. I powdered it. I didn't want someone to have to smell a stinky foot all day.

BEVERLY. The scent: it's really quite lovely.

ADDIE. Thank you.

BEVERLY. My daughter-in-law *is* a nasty little piece of work, isn't she?

ADDIE. Yes.

BEVERLY. I'd prefer her dead.

(A beat.)

ADDIE. What does she do to *you*?

BEVERLY. Keeps me from seeing my grandson.

ADDIE. Ever?

BEVERLY. Unsupervised. When she isn't around. I am never allowed time with Davy when she isn't there.

ADDIE. But why?

BEVERLY. She think's I'm a bad influence.

ADDIE. Why on earth would she say *that?*

BEVERLY. I'll admit it, Addie. I do have bad days. But Debbie acts like all my days are bad days, and that simply isn't true. She says my negative outlook has become "disturbingly harmful for the child." I know I'm not little Mary Sunshine right now, but I do make a point of being as pleasant as possible around my grandson. But she's got her teeth into this thing and she's not going to let it go until I am totally removed from that child's life. I see her plan. *(Looking about.)* Where the hell *is* everybody? *(Considering Addie.)* Your shoulder pads make you look like you're wearing epaulets. *(ADDIE touches her shoulders self-consciously.)* I think we should leave. You're right. Nobody wants to see a woman getting a shoe fitting when they can visit Grauman's Chinese Theatre and the fall of Saigon.

ADDIE. You mean — really — just *go*? *(BEVERLY nods.)* But what about your talk with your son?

BEVERLY. It's not going to do any good. I know that now. Any confrontation is only going to make things worse. Debbie will get her way. Debbie will get her way because Debbie always gets her way and I don't know why he married her, frankly. I cannot see — *(She stops herself.)* Oh look at me. Addie, would you like to know something very interesting? *(ADDIE nods, curious.)* I don't open up like this. To anyone. Ever.

ADDIE. This is a good thing, right?

BEVERLY. I *think* it is.

ADDIE. You should call me.

BEVERLY. Yes, I should. *(Beat.)* Be careful, though, what you wish for.

ADDIE. Oh stop.

BEVERLY. *(Mischievous.)* I could end up calling you every day. I could make your life utterly miserable.

ADDIE. I enjoy talking to you, Beverly. I don't think this would ever be a problem. *(Beat.)* I was really upset with you for a while.

BEVERLY. Yes. I know. I'm sorry.

ADDIE. I'm glad we were able to patch things up.

BEVERLY. *(Tenderly.)* Me too. *(Beat.)* Addie. I have to say something. *(She notices the approach of promenaders.)* Damn!

(The two WOMEN freeze. A MAN and WOMAN ENTER quickly. They breeze through, apparently en route to some other gallery. They glance over at Beverly and Addie.)

MAN. Wartime. Shoes. Got it.

WOMAN. *(Singing.)* "Pardon me boys, is that the Chattanooga shoe shoe?"

(They both EXIT, laughing.)

ADDIE. That was Mr. Duncan. *(Giving a tug to her hair.)* The Propecia seems to be working. You were about to say something.

BEVERLY. Yes. *(She stands up.)* Addie, dear. I don't know how to have a friend.

ADDIE. Even as a little girl, you never had a special playmate?

BEVERLY. *(Shaking her head)* I lived with my grandmother. We made pies. I spent my childhood making pies. I don't remember friends. Just pies. And some childhood obesity issues.

ADDIE. I could teach you. I mean, what little I know.

BEVERLY. I'm an old dog.

ADDIE. And I'm an old dog too. We're a couple of lonely old bitches aren't we? I mean in the dog sense.

BEVERLY. *(Warm laughter.)* I know what you mean.

ADDIE. Let's stick it out, Beverly. Then you can have a long talk with Brian. See if he can't help you and Debbie work this thing out between the two of you. Your son is a genius, honey. Last year he did a circus high wire tableau that had people gasping the second they walked in.

BEVERLY. Yes, I heard it was a real hit.

ADDIE. And when you get to New York, I want you to keep your word.

(SHE gestures "call me.")

BEVERLY. I will. Yes, I will.

(LIGHTS fade out. In the darkness we hear ADDIE and BEVERLY's voice's through a phone filter.)

BEVERLY'S VOICE. Hello?

ADDIE'S VOICE. Beverly?

BEVERLY'S VOICE. Hello, dear. Is anything wrong?

ADDIE'S VOICE. Why do you think that something's wrong?

BEVERLY'S VOICE. Because we just spoke this morning.

ADDIE'S VOICE. Everything's fine. *(Beat.)* I think. I mean that I just called to tell you that I did it. I went right ahead and turned in my two weeks notice. I was in the middle of helping a customer and I said, "Excuse me, sir. I'll be back in just a moment. I have to turn in my resignation." Two weeks from now I am officially retired.

BEVERLY'S VOICE. I'm so proud of you, Addie. So what are you going to do now?

ADDIE'S VOICE. I don't know. I don't know *what* I'm going to do.

BEVERLY'S VOICE. Well, you can always come see me in New York.

ADDIE'S VOICE. Yes, and you can always make an extra trip or two to Dix.

BEVERLY'S VOICE. I should, Addie. Now that Brian and Debbie are separated, it's such a lovely town to visit!

(LIGHTS bump on. The tableau is this: Thelma and Louise's convertible suspended in the air at about a 45 degree angle — frozen in mid-plummet off the cliff. ADDIE, dressed as Thelma, sits behind the wheel; BEVERLY, dressed as Louise, sits next to her. Both of their mouths are locked in a suspended scream, their arms up in the air roller coaster style. TWO WOMEN stand staring up at them.)

FIRST WOMAN. Which one's Thelma, which one's Louise?

SECOND WOMAN. I think Thelma is the one behind the steering wheel.

FIRST WOMAN. They look like they're enjoying themselves.

SECOND WOMAN. They're "empowered."

FIRST WOMAN. But they're about to die.

SECOND WOMAN. That's their choice. It's about choices.

FIRST WOMAN. Well, I don't choose to look at it anymore. (SHE starts off.) I'm going to the Roman chariot race.

SECOND WOMAN. Wait a minute. Are you saying this tableau sends the wrong message?

(The FIRST WOMAN stops and turns around.)

FIRST WOMAN. I'm saying it sends a *horrible* message. That the only way a woman can take control of her life is by ending it.

(SHE turns and exits. A MAN enters.)

MAN. *(Gawking at the tableau.)* Boy howdy!

SECOND WOMAN. *(Recognizing the man.)* Is that *you*, Charlie O'Shaunessy?

MAN. Veronica Parker! Good Lord in the morning, I haven't seen you since high school.

SECOND WOMAN. Graduation. We were seated right to each other. Don't you remember?

MAN (Grinning.) Of course I remember. So where have you been keeping yourself all these years?

SECOND WOMAN. Right here in Dix. Two marriages. Three children. Literacy Council. I also feed the hungry.

MAN. You look fantastic.

SECOND WOMAN. And you're not looking too shabby yourself, sir.

MAN. I was on my way to the chariot race. Have you seen it yet?

SECOND WOMAN. The line was too long earlier. But I'm willing to give it another shot.

(THEY start to stroll out.)

MAN. My God, Ronnie, you are looking so fine.

SECOND WOMAN. Nobody has called me Ronnie since high school. *(Beat; a wink.)* And please don't stop.

(They EXIT. ADDIE and BEVERLY drop their arms. Both release a collective "whew!")

BEVERLY. I have absolutely no circulation in my hands.

ADDIE. Let me rub them for you. *(ADDIE begins briskly rubbing BEVERLY's hands.)* So when did the divorce become final?

BEVERLY. Week before last.

ADDIE. I didn't hear about it, but then I'm not hearing much of anything these days.

BEVERLY. You should get out more.

ADDIE. I'm trying, Bev. I really am. *(Beat.)* How is he handling it?

BEVERLY. As well as he can. I think he still loves her. I don't know why. But he does. Thank you. *(She retrieves her hands and begins to stretch and flex her arms. ADDIE does the same.)* Anyway, Brian's got other troubles. *(ADDIE leans in.)* Here in the museum. Oh, Addie, he's gotten himself into such hot water with the board.

ADDIE. Over what?

BEVERLY. What do you think? Note that we are seated in a convertible that has just gone off the side of a cliff. The Dix Tableaux have become the Dix Circus Maximus. They had a big meeting this morning.

ADDIE. On "Tableau Day"?

BEVERLY. What better day to collect all the evidence? But it makes absolutely no sense. There are people lined up down the street to get into this building. The museum's taking in so much money, it's obscene.

ADDIE. They bought a Kinkade last week.

BEVERLY. And yet in spite of this, Brian's job's on the line. They're saying that he's made a mockery of the tableaux. That these tableaux no longer honor the history of the town. They are saying,

Addie, that the tableaux now only serve to honor the creative ingenuity of Brian Duggins. He's not in a good position.

ADDIE. I'll admit that the tableaus aren't what they used to be, but then this *town* isn't what it used to be. Everything changes. And I just happen to have grown to like the new tableaus. They're fun. They're... *dynamic*. Look at this. Look at *us*. We're movie stars. I feel like a movie star, Beverly. I couldn't wait for tableau weekend this year.

(BEVERLY smiles and pats ADDIE's hand affectionately.)

BEVERLY. Me too. But that was only half the reason.

(ADDIE returns her smile.)

ADDIE. Who do you think they would get to replace him?

BEVERLY. He said there's been talk that the job might go to someone by the name of Gleason.

ADDIE. Oh my good Lord. Not Jaston Gleason.

BEVERLY. This is not a good thing?

ADDIE. Oh it's a terrible thing. Jaston Gleason would take us all the way back to the Stone Age.

BEVERLY. Do you mean that literally or figuratively?

ADDIE. Oh, literally, honey. Before Brian came on board, Jaston tried to get Mr. Creel to do a prehistorical thing with all the tableaus having to do with cave men and woolly mammoths, and oh, Beverly, all of his ideas — they were so *awful!*

BEVERLY. Woolly mammoths?

ADDIE. *(Nodding.)* He said that before Dix was built here, this land was occupied by the red man, and before the red man there were a prehistoric people here called "the children of the moon." They hunted wild game by moonlight and gathered nuts and wild rice by day.

BEVERLY. How do you know so much about this man?

ADDIE. *(After a beat, a reluctant admission.)* I went out on a date with him.

BEVERLY. Oh Addie, *really?*

ADDIE. I haven't *always* kept to myself, Beverly. After Carl died, I went out a few times. I just couldn't find anyone who even came close to Carl.

BEVERLY. So you stopped looking.

ADDIE. Yes.

BEVERLY. They were all like Jaston Gleason?

ADDIE. Some were worse. I am not lucky in love, Beverly. Once I was very lucky, but that was many —

BEVERLY. *(Noticing approaching promenaders, interrupting.)* Battle stations!

(BEVERLY and ADDIE's hands go back up in the air. Their expressions return to silent screams. A WOMAN ENTERS. SHE stands, studying the tableau. A moment later a little GIRL runs in. The tableau stops her in her tracks.)

WOMAN. Vanessa. Don't stand so close. The car could fall down on you.

GIRL. What are they doing, Aunt Becky?

WOMAN. They've driving off a cliff, dear.

GIRL. What's going to happen to them?

WOMAN. We'll, they're going to die, sweetie. They're going to crash into the bottom of the canyon and their car is probably going to blow up in a fireball.

(Hearing this, the GIRL becomes noticeably upset.)

GIRL. *(Hardly getting the words out.)* A big fireball?

WOMAN. I would think so. It will be a tragedy. But that's life. *(The GIRL is now paralyzed with a mixture of fear and sudden despondence.)* So what does this teach us, Vanessa? *(The GIRL shakes her head, tears welling up in her eyes.)* That you should always buckle your seat belt? *(The GIRL nods tentatively.)* Because do you see seat belts or shoulder straps on these two women?

GIRL. No.

WOMAN. And what are you going to do the *next* time I ask you to do a simple thing like buckle your seat belt?

GIRL. Buckle my seat belt?

WOMAN. *(Nodding.)* That's right. And what do we buckle up for?

GIRL. For safety?

WOMAN. Exactly. That's a good girl. Don't you love these outings with your Aunt Becky?

GIRL. I guess.

(THEY walk out. ADDIE and BEVERLY relax their expressions and lower their hands.)

ADDIE. That was cruel.

BEVERLY. It certainly got the message across, "boy howdy"! *(ADDIE stares off, her mind suddenly captured by a thought.)* Addie? Addie, dear?

ADDIE. Yes?

BEVERLY. Are you all right?

ADDIE. I was thinking about my little boy. I do that. Oh goodness. "Little boy." He'd be almost thirty-eight now. I can't even picture that. I heard about this computer place where they can take a child's picture and age it. They can put any number of years on the face. Do you think I should have them do that to Owen?

BEVERLY. I don't know, dear. How do you think it would make you feel?

ADDIE. I don't know. But I *have* always wondered.

(THREE bells ring.)

BEVERLY. Thank God! *(The TWO WOMEN begin to extricate themselves from the car and to climb down through a trap door in the seat behind them. We hear a cell phone RINGING. BEVERLY stops where she is and takes the call. ADDIE climbs on down to the floor, attentive to the call.)* Hello?... So did they make their decision? *(Her face falls.)* That's terrible. That's just terrible, Brian. *(She glances at ADDIE; her face says it all: the ax has fallen.)* Is there a way to appeal it? ... I see... You're so talented, dear, there are museums out there that would snatch you right up. Look, I'll meet you in the lobby in five minutes. I still have to get out of this car. *(She puts the phone away. To ADDIE.)* They want it the way it used to be.

(SHE starts to climb down.)

ADDIE. Where's he going to go?

BEVERLY. Well, I would imagine that there aren't a lot of museums around that still do these live dioramas.

ADDIE. It doesn't matter. Tableaus aren't the *only* thing Brian does well.

BEVERLY. You're right.

ADDIE. But it still isn't fair.

ADDIE. *(Seized by a horrible thought.)* Oh my God!

BEVERLY. What?

ADDIE. This is our last tableau. You and me. This is it.

BEVERLY. Jaston Gleason is really that bad?

ADDIE. You do not want to be in any tableau which that nut

case dreamed up, believe me.

BEVERLY. I'll miss it, but I suppose I won't miss it as much as you will. Good grief, Addie, just think of all the years you've been coming here.

ADDIE. *(Shrugging.)* Things change. Life is supposed to be about adjusting to change, now, isn't it? Some change is bad. But some change is for the better. Beverly, I don't want to embarrass you, but I'd like to give you a big ol' country-girl-hug right now if that's okay.

BEVERLY. *(A little thrown.)* All right. But why?

ADDIE. *(In an exaggerated hillbilly accent.)* Because I ain't never do'ed it. *(ADDIE embraces BEVERLY. ADDIE begins to cry. BEVERLY'S eyes also moisten.)* Are we having our Thelma and Louise moment?

(ADDIE laughs and nods as LIGHTS FADE OUT. In the darkness we hear ADDIE and BEVERLY's phone-filtered voices.)

BEVERLY'S VOICE. Well, I wanted to see you dear. So, I thought, why not help raise some money for that old art museum?

ADDIE'S VOICE. Oh Beverly, are you sure you want to do this? Who knows what that loon will do to us?

BEVERLY'S VOICE. Aren't you even a little curious about what he's going to come up with?

ADDIE'S VOICE. Beverly, I wasn't going to even look in the window, that's how not-curious I am.

BEVERLY'S VOICE. It'll be fun. I need some fun right now.

ADDIE'S VOICE. And Brian's not even here. You should be going to San Diego to see Brian and Davy.

BEVERLY'S VOICE. But I want to see *you*, Addie. There are very few things in my life that I can count on these days. You and that silly old tableau weekend are just about it, so don't give me any trouble, all right?

ADDIE'S VOICE. All right. But you've been *warned.*

(LIGHTS come up on the front entrance of a cave. Downstage is the semblance of a campfire — perhaps bright red crepe paper fluttering up from a manufactured air stream. ADDIE and BEVERLY, dressed in Neanderthal fashion, are squatting in front of the "fire." Each holds a stick over it. Skewered on each stick appears to be some sort of crispy rodent.)

ADDIE. *(Her expression one of total displeasure.)* Ugh.

BEVERLY. Ugh. Ugh. Ooga ooga.

ADDIE. No. I mean, really: *ugh.*

BEVERLY. It *is* disgusting, isn't it? Are these rats? What kind of vermin is on the end of these sticks?

ADDIE. *(Shrugging.)* All I know is that I've seen pictures of the discovery of fire, and those people do not look like us. We look like monkeys, Beverly. I think he's gotten it all wrong.

BEVERLY. If I have to squat here another minute, I won't be able straighten up for a week.

(SHE sits down on the floor. ADDIE sits down too.)

ADDIE. You're right. This squatting is for the birds. This whole tableau is about the biggest lamebrain idea I've ever seen. I can't believe you wanted to do this.

BEVERLY. It was for old time's sake, Addie. *(Beat.)* Of course, it really isn't *anything* like the others, now is it?

(ADDIE drops her skewer.)

ADDIE. Who would eat this? A cave woman wouldn't eat this.

BEVERLY. *(Examining the rodent)* I think it's a mole. A little baby mole. *(Calmly, almost matter-of-fact.)* The cancer came back.

(ADDIE's face registers shock. She is about to respond as MAUREEN ENTERS.)

MAUREEN. *(Admonishing.)* What are the two of you doing? You're supposed to be squatting on your haunches.

BEVERLY. We can't squat anymore. Our haunches hurt.

MAUREEN. Addie, pick up your stick. Your kebob is now all covered in sawdust. *(ADDIE is still looking at BEVERLY.)* Addie, did you hear me? You simply must cooperate if you want this day to be a success.

ADDIE. *(Turning to look up at MAUREEN.)* Nobody's even coming this year, Maureen. Or haven't you noticed?

MAUREEN. People will come. It's still early. Maybe they just need a little time to adjust to the new regime.

ADDIE. *(To MAUREEN.)* And please, would you mind telling me how on earth you got to be first assistant tableau coordinator? Are you sleeping with the new museum director?

MAUREEN. *That*, Adeline, was entirely out of line. Now get back to squatting. Get back to the way I showed you, *please! (ADDIE and BEVERLY do not budge.)* Don't make me get Mr. Gleason.

BEVERLY. We are cave women who sit, Maureen. We sit and we do not eat.

(MAUREEN stares at the two women. She snorts slightly and, apparently capitulating, EXITS. ADDIE looks at BEVERLY.)

ADDIE. When did you find out?

BEVERLY. They did the biopsy last week. I go into surgery on Thursday.

ADDIE. Why didn't you tell me on the phone?

BEVERLY. Because I wanted to tell you in person. I wanted to tell you while we were in the middle of this silliness. I thought it would take a little of the edge off of it.

ADDIE. What does the doctor say?

BEVERLY. That things could go either way. We have to wait and see.

ADDIE. Does Brian know?

BEVERLY. Not yet.

ADDIE. Why haven't you told him?

BEVERLY. Brian and I aren't really speaking at the moment.

ADDIE. Oh Beverly!

BEVERLY. It will blow over. It was inevitable. He's miserable without Debbie. My son is insane. I don't even know how to talk to him. Enough about Brian. Let's talk about me losing my other breast.

ADDIE. Do you want me to come to New York?

BEVERLY. No, I would not ask you to do that.

ADDIE. Maybe you could come down here? There's a wonderful medical center here in Dix. It serves a three county area.

BEVERLY. *(Grinning.)* Three whole counties! Now, that's got to be one helluva medical center!

ADDIE. Are you making fun of me?

BEVERLY. Yes, country girl, I am making fun of you.

ADDIE. Well — *(Beat.)* Well, you go right ahead and make fun of me if you want to.

BEVERLY. Oh, Addie. Why did you come into my life so late?

ADDIE. It isn't over. Please don't talk like that.

BEVERLY. We could have been lifelong friends.

ADDIE. Yes. I think we could have.

(ADDIE takes BEVERLY's hand.)

BEVERLY. You look so stupid in that outfit.

ADDIE. And I suppose you look like Audrey Hepburn in yours?

(They laugh. A beat.)

BEVERLY. *(Softly.)* Come to New York.

ADDIE. *(Softly and tenderly.)* I will.

(LIGHTS fade out here. In the darkness we hear hospital sounds — paging bells, elevator doors opening and closing, whispered conversations, footsteps on hard floors. LIGHTS come up on a new tableau: a hospital bed. In the bed lies BEVERLY. Next to her sits ADDIE. She holds a magazine loosely in her hands, but she has drifted off, her chin resting on her chest. We hold on this tableau for a long time. Finally, a NURSE ENTERS, transforming the tableau into reality. ADDIE wakens to the sound of the nurse checking on BEVERLY.)

ADDIE. *(In a whisper to the nurse.)* Do you think she needs another pain pill?

NURSE. *(Also whispering.)* She'll let us know. Why don't we let her rest a little longer? *(ADDIE nods.)* I still don't see your cot. Let me find out what happened to it.

(ADDIE nods again. The NURSE goes out. ADDIE gets up and stretches her arms. She moves about, bending her legs a little. BEVERLY wakes up.)

BEVERLY. Addie, can I have a sip of that water there? *(ADDIE takes the drink cup to Beverly and lets her sip some liquid from the straw.)* Thank you. My mouth was so dry I could hardly swallow.

ADDIE. I think that's the medication. Why don't you go back

to sleep?

BEVERLY. I will. *(Beat.)* Where's your cot?

ADDIE. They're trying to find out why it never arrived.

BEVERLY. Why don't you go back to my apartment and get some real rest?

ADDIE. Because I would rather be *here*, so stop asking.

BEVERLY. Which was your favorite?

ADDIE. Which what?

BEVERLY. The tableaux we did.

ADDIE. The very first. The two frontier women.

BEVERLY. That was nothing special.

ADDIE. Still, I liked it.

BEVERLY. "She said, smiling sentimentally."

ADDIE. You stop!

BEVERLY. Are you going to do it?

ADDIE. Do what?

BEVERLY. Are you going to take that new job?

ADDIE. It's just a volunteer position.

BEVERLY. But it sounds like a lot of fun, dear. Mr. Gleason gets to keep running the museum, but the board lets you run the annual tableaus. It sounds like the perfect setup. *(ADDIE is thinking.)* You have wonderful ideas, Addie. You'd be just the right person.

ADDIE. Whatever I decide, I was still very flattered that they even asked.

BEVERLY. You've participated in tableau weekend probably longer than anyone, dear. Not to mention, you are thought of quite highly in that town. Have you ever stopped to think of all the people whose lives you've made just a little bit better through the miracle of pharmacology?

(THEY both start laughing.)

ADDIE. Beverly, you are terrible. *(Beat, then soberly.)* I don't want to do it without you.

BEVERLY. I know you don't, dear. *(Beat.)* But you will.

ADDIE. I will?

BEVERLY. Yes, Addie. Because if you don't, there's the possibility they might give it to Mr. Gleason again and then *nobody* will come. It would be a tragedy. Or even worse, what if it all lands in Maureen's lap? Now wouldn't that be a horror?

(THEY both laugh. BEVERLY closes her eyes from an apparent ripple of pain.)

ADDIE. Do you need another pain pill? Where's the nurse's call button?

(BEVERLY opens her eyes.)

BEVERLY. *(Pushing the button.)* I've got it. *(She closes her eyes again, settling back.)* Addie?

ADDIE. Yes?

BEVERLY. Let's do a tableau.

ADDIE. *(A tiny smile.)* What kind of tableau would you like to do?

BEVERLY. Come sit here next to me. *(ADDIE pulls the chair up next to the bed and sits down.)* Take my hand.

(ADDIE takes Beverly's outstretched hand.)

ADDIE. What should we call it?

BEVERLY. *(After a thought.)* "Friends In Extremis."

ADDIE. What does that mean?

BEVERLY. "Friends to the end."

(LIGHTS fade very slowly to black. We hear an ORGAN playing "Nearer My God to Thee." The MUSIC continues to play as LIGHTS come up on a closed coffin draped with flowers. Slightly downstage are a row of folding chairs. MAUREEN ENTERS dressed in black. She goes to the flowers and adjusts them slightly, then takes a seat in the row of chairs. Another moment or two passes. Other MOURNERS ENTER and take their seats. Finally, ADDIE ENTERS. She is also dressed funereally. She walks up to MAUREEN.)

ADDIE. *(Somberly.)* Hello, Maureen.
MAUREEN. Hello, Addie.
ADDIE. Did you move those flowers?
MAUREEN. Yes. They looked a little askew.
ADDIE. You mean a little askew like you, Maureen? *(MAUREEN doesn't answer. ADDIE goes to the coffin. SHE lifts up the cover. It is empty. ADDIE turns to MAUREEN, alarmed.)* Where is she? *(MAUREEN shrugs. ADDIE calls.)* BEVERLY! BEVERLY!

(BEVERLY comes rushing in. SHE is dressed like a female version of Dracula.)

BEVERLY. *(Apologetic.)* I was in the bathroom.
ADDIE. I thought you were already in the casket.
BEVERLY. I tried it. It was very comfortable. But I had to pee.

(The MALE MOURNER helps BEVERLY up a step stool and into the casket.)

ADDIE. *(To BEVERLY.)* Do you like it?

BEVERLY. I like it, dear.

ADDIE. Is it too "Brian"?

BEVERLY. It's perfect. It's "*Brian-light.*"

ADDIE. I'm so nervous.

BEVERLY. You're going to do just fine. All the tableaus — they're all so wonderful.

(ADDIE smiles. MAUREEN raises her hand.)

MAUREEN. Addie, would you mind if I moved my chair just the teeniest little bit so people could at least see my profile?

ADDIE. Yes, I do mind, Maureen. Now if you can't just sit there like everybody else, I'm going to put you in the Persian market tableau and make you wear a burka.

(The two-minute BELL rings.)

BEVERLY. *(To ADDIE.)* So we get you first?

ADDIE. First and last. And maybe next year when you have *all* your strength back you can make the rounds of all the tableaus with me.

BEVERLY. It sounds absolutely exhausting! *(Beat, then conspiratorially.)* But fun as hell!

ADDIE. *(To All.)* Does anyone need anything? George, your tie is a little crooked.

GEORGE. But nobody's going to even see my tie.

ADDIE. It's all about verisimilitude, George. Mustn't forget the verisimilitude, am I right, Beverly? *(BEVERLY smiles and nods.)* I hear the doors opening. Is everybody ready?

(Nods all around. ADDIE takes her seat with the other "mourners.")

ADDIE. *(Cont.)* And... *tableau!*

(BEVERLY becomes "Draculina," rising from her coffin nap. She bares her teeth in a Vampire's snarl. All of the mourners freeze in outlandish reactive poses of abject fright. It is picture perfect. Tableau.)

THE END

PROPERTY LIST

The following list incorporates only those properties called for by the script. Obviously, the opportunity to dress each tableau as sparsely or as elaborately as needed will be left to the director, designer, and prop master or mistress of each future production.

SCENE ONE (on the frontier)
butter church
broom
hanging rug
cell phone
note pad
pencil

SCENE TWO (The Spit and Curl)
electrified curlers
bottle of Coca-Cola
screen magazine
cigarette
pack of cigarettes
second cigarette

SCENE THREE (Parker's Dairy)
milk pail
pocket book
photograph

SCENE FOUR (Lonely Woman in a Chair)
magazine

DIX TABLEAUX

SCENE FIVE (1950's high school classroom)
pointer

SCENE SIX (shoe store)
cell phone
empty shoeboxes
display shoes

SCENE SEVEN (Thelma and Louise's convertible)
cell phone

SCENE EIGHT (prehistoric times)
two cooked rodents on skewers

SCENE NINE (hospital room)
magazine
water cup and straw

SCENE TEN (funeral parlor)
flowers

NOTE ON SET AND COSTUMES

Because *Dix Tableaux* unfolds through a series of ten separate "tableaux" or human dioramas, the construction, placement, and ultimate realization of each mini-set will be entirely dependent upon the unique demands and exigencies of each venue in which the play is to be performed. Therefore, no definitive collection of set designs accompanies this script. Practically speaking, the author suggests making the mini-sets as mobile as possible. In the premiere production of this play, some of the tableau sets were constructed on rolling platforms, even including Thelma and Louise's plummeting convertible (which garnered gasps and applause at each performance). The idea is to make each tableau as evocative and illustrative of the scene and period it conveys as possible while avoiding lengthy and — for the audience — patience-taxing set changes.

It is left to the costume designer of each new production the challenge of how he or she wishes to enhance the flavor and reality through costume of each of the widely disparate tableaux presented in the play. Some details should be obvious: long pioneer skirts on the frontier-women, "Joan Crawford" shoulder pads for the saleswoman and customer in the World War II-era shoe store, bobby socks on the 1950s teenager and so forth. Designers should enjoy their full license to be as conservative or adventurous in their imaginings as they desire. (Perhaps the stone-age women are dressed as Wilma Flintstone and Betty Rubble!)

The promenaders should all be dressed in color-muted casual-wear appropriate to the recurring season (late spring) to draw a contrast between the pedestrian "real" world and the "fantasy" world of the tableaux.

The Lone Star Love Potion
MICHAEL PARKER

"Another hit for Parker."—*Palm Beach Post*

"Gales of laughter reached hurricane force. This play's a hoot."—*Boca Raton News*

Mr. Stancliff, the owner of a vast fortune and a 200,000-acre Texas ranch, has died. His unflappable butler, an alluring maid, the rancher's only living relative, her husband and the girl next door have gathered to hear the attorney read the will. Acting on the deceased's instructions, the butler produces a sample of what is reputed to be a potent love potion—with hilarious results. The flow of characters in, out and from under the beds reaches a frenetic pace before the truth about the potion is revealed. Anyone who savors uproarious farce, especially fans of the author's *The Amorous Ambassador* and *The Sensuous Senator,* is guaranteed to enjoy this original comedy. 3 m., 4 f. (#14209)

The Marriage Counselor
JOEY OUELLETTE

A traveling vacuum cleaner salesman wanders into a marriage counselor's office. Susan and Tiger burst in, arguing so fiercely that the salesman can't get a word in edge-wise. They mistake him for the marriage counselor and he never gets a chance to enlighten them. Next to arrive are Susan's sister (who is having an affair with Tiger) and a UPS man who is coincidentally Susan's lover. Things get even crazier when another UPS delivery person turns out to be Tiger's first wife who was presumed dead. That's when the man with the gun and a grudge storms in, determined to kill the counselor and everyone else if need be. When things get sorted out, three couples exit happily. 4 m., 3 f. (#15541)